VICTORIA AND LAMBETH TRAMWAYS

Robert J Harley

MP Middleton Press

First published March 1995

ISBN 1 873793 49 9

© Middleton Press 1995

Design - Deborah Goodridge

Published by Middleton Press
            Easebourne Lane
            Midhurst
            West Sussex
            GU29 9AZ
            Tel: 01730 813169

Printed & bound by Biddles Ltd,
            Guildford and Kings Lynn

CONTENTS

GEOGRAPHICAL SETTING

On the southern banks of the River Thames marshland once extended from Southwark to Battersea. An area of isolated settlements, situated mostly on level terrain, has grown over the centuries into a vast urban network.

Ordnance Survey maps are to the scale of 25" to 1 mile.

Other maps used in this book are the work of the late Frank Merton Atkins, who spent a lifetime surveying and walking the tram routes of South London. They are published here as a tribute to his scholarship.

INTRODUCTION AND ACKNOWLEDGEMENTS

This is the final volume of a trilogy devoted to the tramways of inner South London. In this and the other two books, *Southwark and Deptford Tramways* and *Embankment and Waterloo Tramways*, a picture is painted of almost ninety years of tramway operation. Much has changed since 1952 when the last tram graced the streets of South London; new road schemes and housing estates have altered many of the locations featured in the following pages. In recalling this lost world I hope the reader may remember a time when traffic flowed more smoothly and the pace of life was attuned to a more leisurely tempo. South London has suffered at the hands of so called fashionable critics, and the area has also had to endure the wartime depredations of heavy bombing, but the true spirit has survived all these upheavals. The trams dominated the main thoroughfares for many years, thus making this form of transport an important factor in local history.

My thanks go to the photographers who had the foresight to record this bygone age. All lovers of the Capital's past owe them a debt of gratitude in preserving for future generations a glimpse of the lives of South Londoners at work or on the move throughout the first half of the twentieth century.

HISTORICAL BACKGROUND

Lambeth Palace, which is located on the south bank of the Thames, has been for many centuries the main residence of the Arch-bishops of Canterbury. The hinterland was sparsely populated and it only acquired more inhabitants from the early seventeenth century onwards when Londoners from over the water began to look south for their amusements. Vauxhall Gardens were first established in 1615 and they subsequently attracted famous visitors such as Charles II and the diarist Samuel Pepys. Hogarth, the artist with a perceptive eye for contemporary political and social mores, was often to be found amongst "the fragrant gardens and secluded arbours." The area was also the centre of the glass making industry and the Vauxhall Plate Glass Works was in use from 1670 until 1780. It produced goods and artifacts which were said to have rivalled the famous Venetian glasswear of the period. The popularity and reputation of the pleasure gardens began to wane in the early 1800s, by which time other distractions were making their mark. Vauxhall Bridge opened in 1816 thus effecting better communication across the Thames; further strides in transport were heralded by the arrival of the London and Southampton Railway in 1838. The temporary terminus at Nine Elms was superseded by an extension to Waterloo in 1848.

Street tramways entered the scene with a short lived experiment constructed by George Francis Train; the rails from the south side of Westminster Bridge along Kennington Road to Kennington turnpike gate lasted from

August 1861 to June 1862. A more successful venture, the Metropolitan Street Tramways Co. constructed a line along Brixton Road to the Horns Tavern, Kennington in 1870; from then on tramway expansion proceeded apace. Kennington Road was again laid with tram tracks and services were also started by the Pimlico, Peckham and Greenwich Street Tramways Co. from Vauxhall to Camberwell in 1872 and from the north side of Vauxhall Bridge to the Windsor Castle Inn by Victoria Station. A horse bus provided the connection across the bridge for a fare of one halfpenny. It is worth noting that the tracks constructed in 1873 the length of Vauxhall Bridge Road were never permitted to cross the bridge. Attitudes to tramways from the wealthy residents of the West End were almost always hostile and even when the London County Council succeeded in joining the Victoria section to the rest of the electrified network, through lines across the heart of the Capital never materialised. Thus, although the Vauxhall Bridge Road tramway was situated north of the river, it was always regarded for operational reasons as part of the South London network.

London's only standard gauge cable tramway was inaugurated in 1892 with the Kennington to Streatham line. The changeover point from cable to horse was situated at the northern end of Brixton Road. Mechanical rail traction had also appeared in the shape of the City and South London electric tube railway, the first in the world; stations were opened at

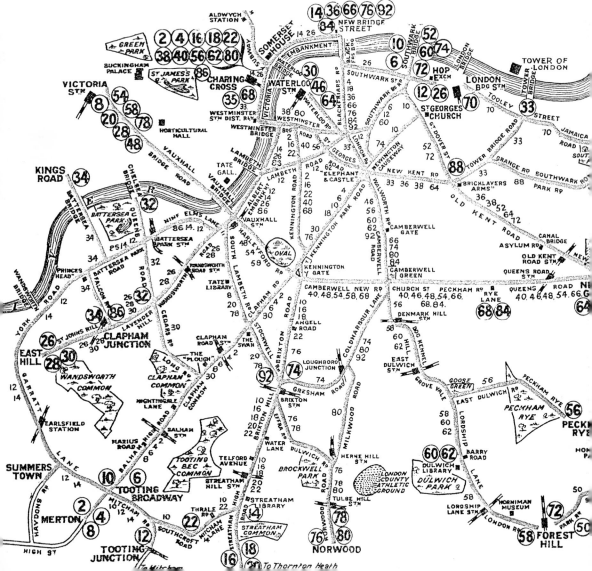

Kennington, the Oval and Stockwell in November 1890. Electric tramways using the underground conduit method of current collection became a common sight from 1903 as the progressive LCC replaced all the horse cars. In three years all the major roads were traversed by new tramcars which offered frequent and cheap local transport. At first open top double deck cars were used, but it was soon found that the inclement climate of the metropolis was better suited to covered tops, and the standard lake maroon and cream LCC trams soon became a familiar feature of local life. Trailers were attached to service cars on some routes around the First World War, but their success was limited and the LCC turned their minds to improving the fleet with more comfortable seats and higher powered motors so that they could fight back against motor bus competition. Citizens of Lambeth were able to reach the outlying suburbs and even the fields of rural Kent and Surrey for a few pence and a single change of tram. The tramcar was the servant of the people, a popular and reliable form of transport in all weathers.

Storm clouds appeared on the horizon in 1933 with the formation of the London Passenger Transport Board which took over all the former LCC tramways, as well as other company and municipal lines in the metropolitan area. It was obvious that the tram was out of favour, it was blamed for traffic congestion and for being inflexible in catering

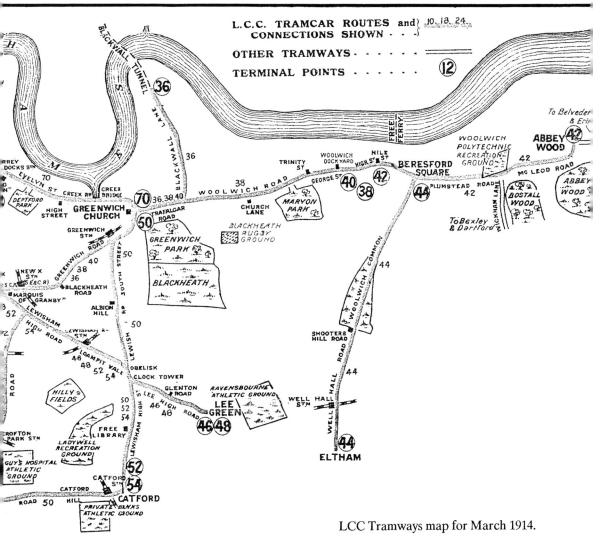

LCC Tramways map for March 1914.

for the needs of the travelling public. The new board, known as London Transport, began a policy of trolleybus substitution for tramways. However, some improvements to the tramways were effected, most notably the traffic scheme at Vauxhall in 1938 which involved new trackwork and the rerouting the local tram services. The intervention of the Second World War halted the conversion programme and the faithful South London trams soldiered on. Many local inhabitants preferred to ride on the trams as the sound and motion of the cars tended to drown out the noise of the bombing and to mask the mayhem going on all around.

The end came in stages as diesel buses of the RT and RTL type started to supplant tramcars from September 1950. The final trams on services 40 and 72 passed through the area on 5th July 1952. An era of environmentally friendly public transport was brought to a conclusion. We are left to ponder the wisdom of the decisions made by London Transport in the light of the traffic congestion which has strangled and polluted South London ever since that sad day in 1952.

1. Victoria

1.   Victoria Station is one of the gateways to London's West End and theatreland. At the Victoria Palace on this November day in 1950, the Crazy Gang are on stage. In the more mundane world, car 170 on service 20 stands at the end of the track at Victoria terminus. The tramways brought much patronage to the clubs and cinemas of the West End.
(D.A.Thompson)

2. The bus routes passing along Vauxhall Bridge Road had free access to the centre of London, but tramway expansion plans were always thwarted by powerful vested interests. This last day scene on 5th January 1952 features car 1991 preparing to return to West Norwood. The replacing buses on the following day would have to execute a turn across the carriageway behind the photographer. (J.C.Gillham)

3. Car 132 approaches cautiously as the marks in the roadway indicate that at least one of its sisters has come to grief at this location. Minor derailments could sometimes be treated by the crew with the aid of hand tools and application of power from the controller. More serious incidents had to await the arrival of a breakdown gang with chains and jacks to budge the stricken vehicle. (D.A.Thompson)

4.   The first Feltham type cars started to appear at Victoria from November 1936, when the services they normally operated in North London went over to trolleybuses. Here two examples of these splendid machines bask in the sunshine before returning to the southern suburbs. (G.Druce)

5.   In order to relieve congestion at the terminus which saw around 180 trams arriving per hour, another loading island for services 54, 58 and 66 was opened in August 1949. Car 2150 makes its way to the northern island past the compulsory stop sign for service 58. (D.Trevor Rowe)

6.   We begin our journey along Vauxhall Bridge Road in company with car 1971 outbound to Grove Park on 9th December 1951. LCC electric trams began operating over this stretch in 1906. (J.H.Meredith)

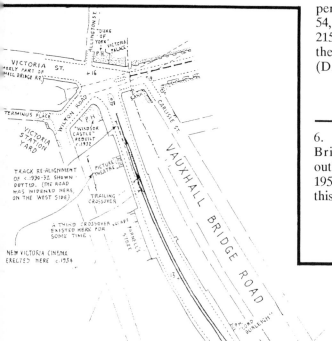

7. After 1914 the LCC reconstructed some lines to include space for pedestrian refuges between the tracks. Here on Vauxhall Bridge Road by Rochester Row an island has been placed to help people cross the road in safety. Everyone seems to be muffled up against the cold on this January day in 1952. Some of the period advertisements on the wall above Attenborough's will remind readers of post-war rationing of sweets. (J.H.Meredith)

8. In the autumn of 1940 the German assault on London got going in earnest with day and night bombing raids - the beginning of the "blitz." Extensive damage was caused at the junction of Vauxhall Bridge Road and Moreton Street. However, repairs went ahead quickly and one track has already been reinstated. (R.J.Harley Coll.)

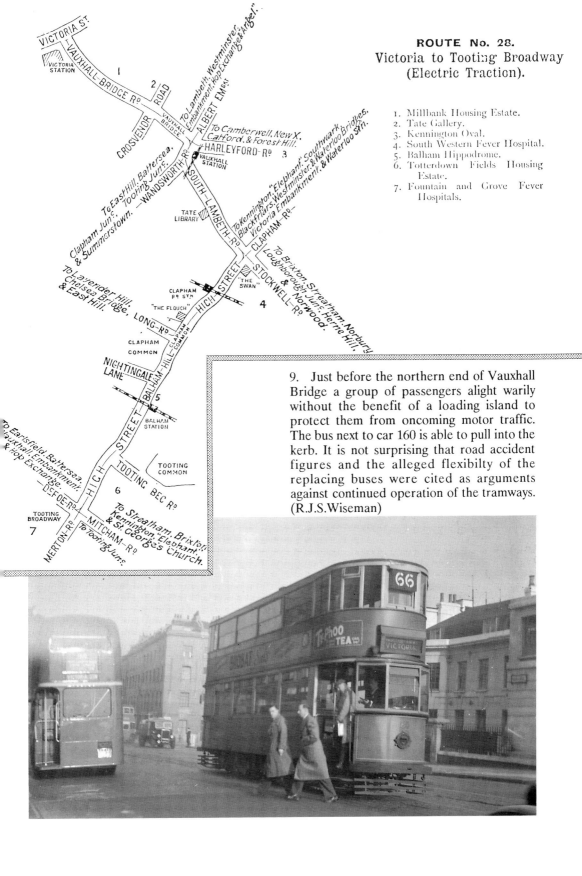

VICTORIA ST.

VICTORIA STATION

VAUXHALL-BRIDGE RD

CROSVENOR ROAD

To Lambeth, Westminster, Embankment, Hop Exchange, &c.

ALBERT EMBT

VAUXHALL BRIDGE

To Camberwell, New X. Catford, & Forest Hill.

HARLEYFORD RD

VAUXHALL STATION

To East Hill, Battersea, Clapham Junc, Tooting Junc, & Summerstown.

To Lavender Hill, Chelsea Bridge, & East Hill.

SOUTH-LAMBETH RD

WANDSWORTH RD

TATE LIBRARY

To Kennington, "Elephant," Southwark, Blackfriars, Westminster, & Waterloo Bridges, Victoria Embankment, & Waterloo Stn.

CLAPHAM RD

HIGH STREET

STOCKWELL RD

"THE SWAN"

CLAPHAM RD STN

"THE PLOUGH"

CLAPHAM COMMON

To Brixton, Streatham, Norbury, Loughborough Junc, Herne Hill, & Norwood.

LONG RD

NIGHTINGALE LANE

BALHAM HILL

CLAPHAM-COMMON

BALHAM STATION

TOOTING COMMON

BALHAM HIGH STREET

To Earlsfield, Battersea, Vauxhall Embankment, & Hop Exchange.

TOOTING BEC RD

TOOTING HIGH STREET

DEFOE RD

MERTON RD

MITCHAM RD

TOOTING BROADWAY

To Streatham, Brixton, Kennington, "Elephant," & St. George's Church.

To Tooting Junc.

1. Millbank Housing Estate.
2. Tate Gallery.
3. Kennington Oval.
4. South Western Fever Hospital.
5. Balham Hippodrome.
6. Totterdown Fields Housing Estate.
7. Fountain and Grove Fever Hospitals.

9. Just before the northern end of Vauxhall Bridge a group of passengers alight warily without the benefit of a loading island to protect them from oncoming motor traffic. The bus next to car 160 is able to pull into the kerb. It is not surprising that road accident figures and the alleged flexibilty of the replacing buses were cited as arguments against continued operation of the tramways. (R.J.S.Wiseman)

2. Vauxhall

10. The original Vauxhall Bridge was reconstructed in 1898-1906 and electric car services were delayed for a couple of months in the summer of 1906 whilst the LCC acquired the necessary running rights from Parliament. This last day scene shows car 982 performing one of its final journeys. (D.Trevor Rowe)

11. On the new Vauxhall Bridge special girders were inserted to support the double tram tracks and associated conduit electrical equipment. On this fine Edwardian day you can almost hear the clip-clop of the horse traffic interspersed with the growl of the traction motors as a laden tramcar breasts the brow of the bridge. (J.B.Gent Coll.)

12. New Year 1951 and the situation looks bleak. In London the tramway abandonment programme is about to claim its next victim service 20 seen here at Bridgefoot near Vauxhall Cross. Whilst British Cement may have been conquering the world, the news from other parts of the globe matched the gloom of the weather. In the Korean War advances were reported on all fronts by North Korean and Chinese troops. (R.J.S.Wiseman)

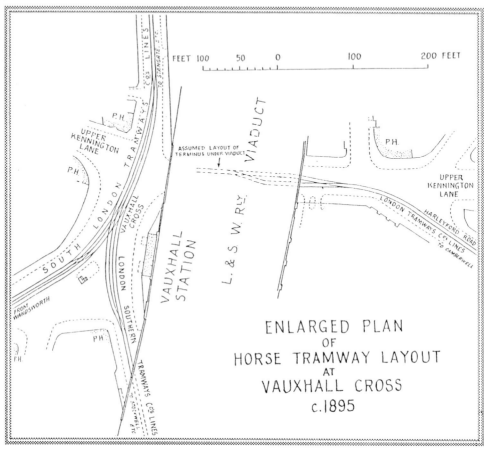

ENLARGED PLAN
OF
HORSE TRAMWAY LAYOUT
AT
VAUXHALL CROSS
c.1895

FEET 100   50   0   100   200 FEET

SOUTH LONDON TRAMWAYS Co'S LINES

TO STANGATE, &c.

UPPER
KENNINGTON
LANE

P.H.

P.H.

ASSUMED LAYOUT OF
TERMINUS UNDER VIADUCT

L. & S. W. RLY. VIADUCT

P.H.

UPPER
KENNINGTON
LANE

VAUXHALL
CROSS

VAUXHALL STATION

LONDON SOUTHERN

LONDON TRAMWAYS Co'S LINES

HARLEYFORD ROAD

TO CAMBERWELL

FROM
WANDSWORTH

P.H.

P.H.

TRAMWAYS Co'S LINES

13. We are looking from Bridgefoot past the waiting tram to Harleyford Road which begins under the bridge carrying the main line to Waterloo Station. Note the temporary police traffic light in front of the tramway section box number 903; the smaller box contains a telephone. (J.C.Gillham)

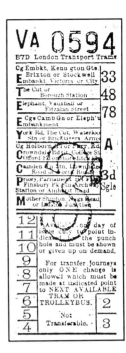

14. At Vauxhall Cross the carriageway is being dug up in February 1906 to receive the heavier rails and conduit needed for the new electric trams. A horse car on borrowed time waits for passengers before taking the tracks along South Lambeth Road in the direction of Stockwell and Brixton. (J.H.Price Coll.)

15. Six years on from the previous view and much has changed on street level. LCC trams dominate the junction of South Lambeth Road with Wandsworth Road outside Vauxhall Station. Straight ahead lies the Albert Embankment; the trams crossing in the centre are on the Harleyford Road, Upper Kennington Lane (Bridgefoot) axis.
(LCC official view)

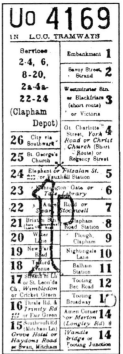

Uo 4169

IN L.C.C. TRAMWAYS

Services
2·4, 6,
8-20,
2a·4a·
22-24
(Clapham
Depot)

Service	Destination	Destination	No.
	Embankment		1
	Savoy Street, Strand		2
	Westminster Stn. or Blackfriars (short route) or Victoria		3
26	City via Southwark	Gt. Charlotte Street, York Road or Christ Church (Short Route) or Regency Street	4
25	St. George's Church		
24	Elephant or Fitzalan St. and or Vauxhall Station		5
23	Kennington Gate or Tate Library		6
22	Akerman Road or Stockwell		7
21	Brixton Stn. (part of route)	Clapham Road Station	8
20	Water Lane	Plough, Clapham	9
19	New Park Road	Nightingale Lane	10
18	Telford Avenue	Balham Station	11
17	Streatham Lib. or St. Leon'ds Ch., Wimbledon or Cricket Green	Tooting Bec Road	12
16	Thrale Rd. & Trinity Rd. or Fair Green	Tooting Broadway	13
15	Southcroft Rd (Mitcham Ln.) Grove Hotel or Haydons Road or Swan, Mitcham	Amen Corner or Merton (Longley Rd)	14
		Wandle Bridge or Tooting Junction	14

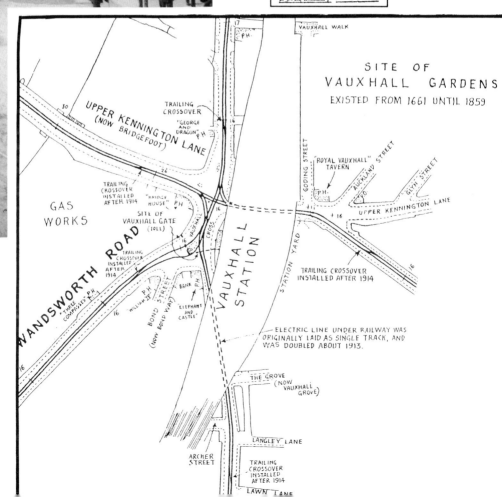

SITE OF
VAUXHALL GARDENS
EXISTED FROM 1661 UNTIL 1859

16. The electric layout here was fully operational from April 1908. In the hustle and bustle of rush hour, note that the driver of the nearest tram with Tooting Broadway on the destination blind, has put up the FULL sign to warn would-be passengers. (LCC official view)

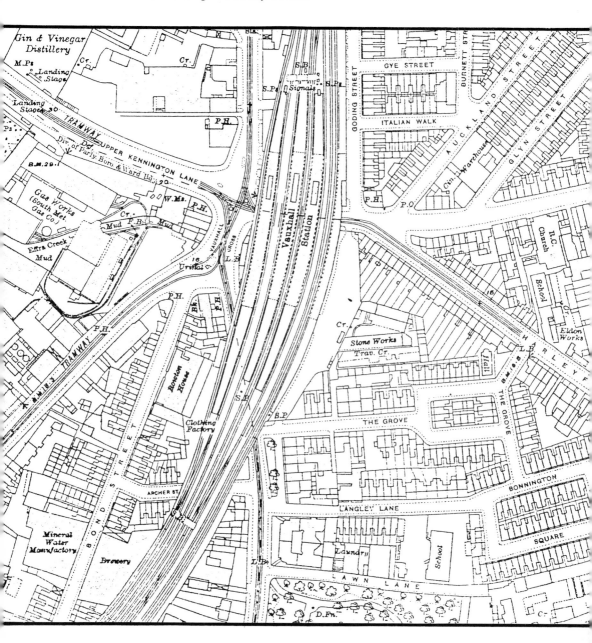

17. Time marches on to August 1936 and the LT regime holds sway over London's tramways. The neighbouring railway lines have been electrified and plans were already in place to turn this whole area into a one way traffic system. (London Transport)

18. A further view taken in the early LT era depicts another, less famous, Elephant and Castle pub by the railway bridge, as a car on service 8 emerges pursued by a tail of motor vehicles. (R.J.Harley Coll.)

19. We return to ground level to share this pre-First World War view with the photographer who is standing at the entrance to South Lambeth Road. (J.B.Gent Coll.)

20. A few steps on from the previous photo-graph and we are in Wandsworth Road. In the foreground a South London Tramways Co. horse car is about to depart for Wandsworth. This service began in 1883 and electric working via Nine Elms Lane commenced in December 1906 with the rest of Wandsworth Road being converted in September 1909. (J.H.Price Coll.)

21. The date is June 1946 and the tracks have been altered in the 1938 reconstruction of Vauxhall Cross and its approach roads. Both these trams are going away from the camera on the "up" lines for the Albert Embankment (car 1312) and Vauxhall Bridge (the Feltham type car). (G.F.Ashwell)

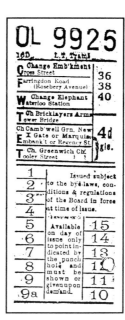

22. A final look at the splayed tracks in Wandsworth Road reveals car 1862 parked on a enthusiasts' special in April 1951. The line it is occupying was not then in regular use, but had been retained in case emergency rerouting of services was necessary. (J.H.Meredith)

23. We are looking north along the line of South Lambeth Road. On the left of the garage is the new road named Parry Street and to the right a highway has been constructed to join Harleyford Road. In this 1938 panorama can be glimpsed both steam and electric trains plus the LT tramcar and motor bus.
(J.H.Price Coll.)

24. The pointsman under the bridge has just switched car 1949 on to the southbound track outside the Royal Vauxhall Tavern in Harleyford Road. Railway milk tank wagons discharged their contents into a bottling plant housed in the arches. (D.A.Thompson)

25. The crew of snowbroom 020 survey the rather chilly surroundings as they inch their way forward clearing the ice from the rails in February 1948. (Lens of Sutton)

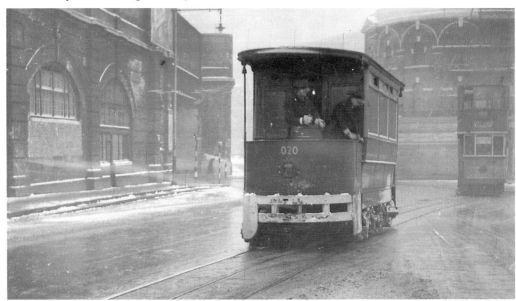

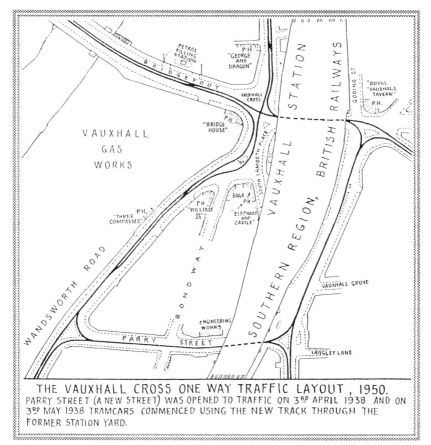

THE VAUXHALL CROSS ONE WAY TRAFFIC LAYOUT, 1950.
PARRY STREET (A NEW STREET) WAS OPENED TO TRAFFIC ON 3RD APRIL 1938 AND ON 3RD MAY 1938 TRAMCARS COMMENCED USING THE NEW TRACK THROUGH THE FORMER STATION YARD.

26. On the south side of Vauxhall roundabout, car 2056 is about to give the competing vehicles from the LT bus department a run for their money. This tram, formerly owned by Walthamstow Corporation was part of a batch nicknamed "rockets" by enthusiasts, they were generally acknowledged to be the fastest members of the post-war fleet. (D.A.Thompson)

27. Sometimes progress came to a halt when, as here, the motorman had to get down to change the points. This was all part of tramway mystique. (J.H.Meredith)

28. Parry Street is completely devoid of traffic save for car 1962 on its journey from North London to Wandsworth via the Kingsway Subway. (D.A.Thompson)

Pi 4620
SE LITTLE

1	8-20	20
2	10	19
3	16-18	18
4	2a-4a	17
	22-24	
	42	
5		16
5a	Streatham and	15
6	Thornton Heath-	14a
6a	spot	14
7	Issued subject to the bye-laws conditions and regulations in force at the time of issue.	13a
8		13
9		12a
9a		12
10	1½d. & 2d	11a
10a	1d Child	11

30. Car 1653 swings into Wandsworth Road after having negotiated Parry Street. (D.A.Thompson)

29. The trams had to be maintained in the 1940s and early 1950s even though their life expectancy was somewhat limited; the same applied to the trackwork, with an example here in Parry Street of repair work taking place. Note the setts piled up at the side of the road waiting to be repacked next to the running rails and the conduit slot rails. (A.J.Watkins)

1938.—VAUXHALL IMPROVEMENT.

Notice to Drivers and Conductors.

Until further notice, up trams on Routes Nos. 12, 14, 26 and 31 will use the Turn Out in Wandsworth Road opposite Clark's passage and proceed to Vauxhall Headway on the offside track, where they will take the new " Swing-over " to the " Up " Albert Embankment track.

Drivers must see that the points in Wandsworth Road are correctly set for the " Offside " track.

All other services will continue normal operation.

3. Albert Embankment,
Lambeth Palace

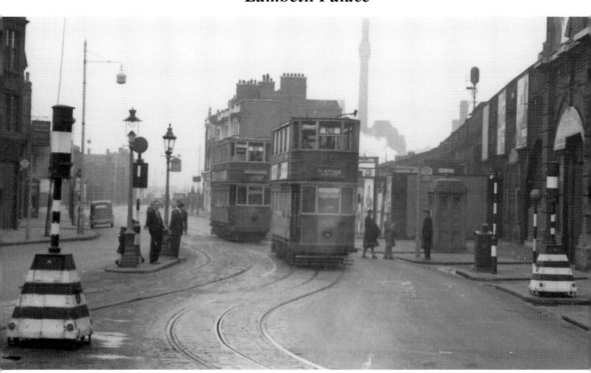

31. Proceeding a little way north from Vauxhall Cross we observe two trams at the entrance to the Albert Embankment. This bunching of service 26 cars can perhaps be excused as the date is 30th September 1950, and the next day buses on route 168 will run as replacements. (J.H.Meredith)

32. Continuing the last day theme, car 2102 is seen on 6th January 1951 outside the George and Dragon. Service 24 is about to pass into history and the sound of tramcars on the Albert Embankment will become a fond memory. (J.H.Meredith)

33. The Royal Albert Embankment, as it was first named, was part of a grand scheme for riverside improvements to the banks of the Thames. Construction started in 1866 and the thoroughfare was completed three years later. To the right of the tram is the HQ of the London Fire Brigade, and to the left in the distance is the well known shape of Big Ben and the Houses of Parliament. (D.A.Thompson)

34. Outside the original Doulton's Lambeth Pottery, car 201 slows for the crossover. The rather eccentric looking stone columns in the background mark the start of Lambeth Bridge. (J.H.Meredith)

LAMBETH CHURCH AND PALACE, THE LONDON RESIDENCE OF THE ARCHBISHOP OF CANTERBURY.

35. Lambeth Bridge in its first 1862 form was described as the ugliest bridge on the Thames. Thankfully it was replaced by the version depicted here, which was opened by King George V in July 1932. The tram is still in wartime garb with white painted fender. (J.H.Price Coll.)

36. Harry Williams in his 1949 book on South London makes the following observation: "Lambeth Palace...the bustling life around it now, the trams which clank the length of its western wall, the children who shout at play in the Archbishop's Park, the never-ending stream of river craft passing and repassing its castellated gateway..." (J.H.Price Coll.)

37. St.Mary's Church by Lambeth Palace is the last resting place of Admiral Bligh, the celebrated captain of *HMS Bounty*. The horse car service outside the Palace dates from 1883; in the middle of the road the two workmen seem about to start a mutiny all by themselves as the well dressed couple on the left watch the altercation. (J.B.Gent Coll.)

39. The late 1920s and Lambeth Palace Road is the setting for this LCC tramcar which belongs to class D. The chap on the top deck enjoying his pipe reminds us that smoking was only permitted in the upper saloon; many trams bore nicotine stains on the upper deck ceiling. (G.N.Southerden)

38. A view dated September 1903 shows the imposing entrance to Lambeth Palace. Three years before electrification of these tracks, the vehicles in the picture are exclusively equine powered. (J.H.Price Coll.)

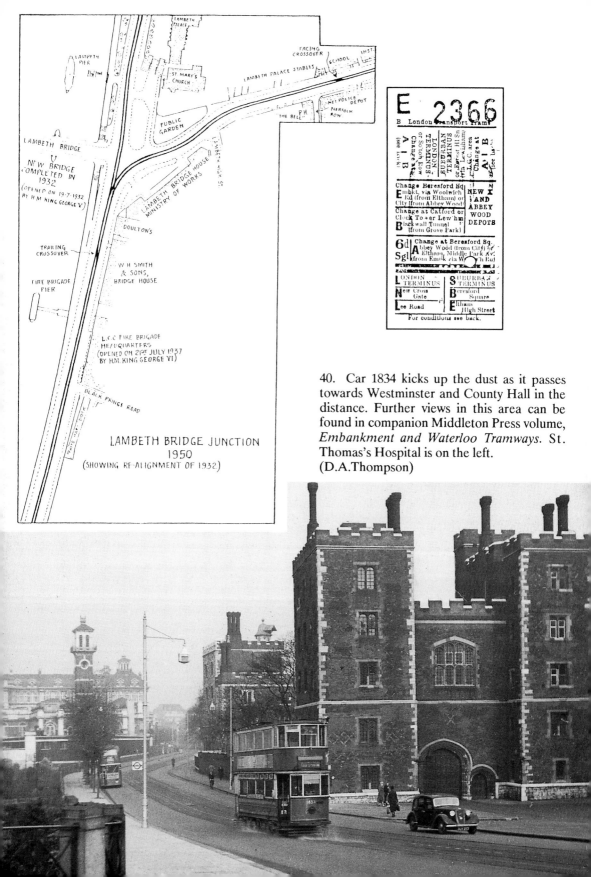

LAMBETH PIER
Pier Head

LAMBETH PALACE

ST. MARY'S CHURCH

FACING CROSSOVER

LAMBETH PALACE STABLES

SCHOOL INST

MET POLICE DEPOT

NORFOLK ROW

THE BELL P.H.

PUBLIC GARDEN

LAMBETH BRIDGE

NEW BRIDGE COMPLETED IN 1932
(OPENED ON 19·7·1932 BY H.M. KING GEORGE V)

LAMBETH BRIDGE HOUSE MINISTRY OF WORKS

LAMBETH HIGH ST

DOULTON'S

TRAILING CROSSOVER

FIRE BRIGADE PIER

W H SMITH & SONS, BRIDGE HOUSE

L.C.C FIRE BRIGADE HEADQUARTERS
(OPENED ON 21ST JULY 1937 BY H.M. KING GEORGE VI)

BLACK PRINCE ROAD

WHITE HART DOCK

LAMBETH BRIDGE JUNCTION
1950
(SHOWING RE-ALIGNMENT OF 1932)

40. Car 1834 kicks up the dust as it passes towards Westminster and County Hall in the distance. Further views in this area can be found in companion Middleton Press volume, *Embankment and Waterloo Tramways*. St. Thomas's Hospital is on the left. (D.A.Thompson)

4. Nine Elms

41. South of Vauxhall, tramlines extended along Wandsworth Road and Nine Elms Lane. At the junction of the two thoroughfares car 1824 pauses to pick up passengers. (J.H.Meredith)

42. At the beginning of Nine Elms Lane the motorman of car 1773 checks to see all is clear before joining the tracks in Wandsworth Road. (D.A.Thompson)

43. Car 200 makes progress along Wandsworth Road in the days before zebra stripes were added to pedestrian crossings. Tram services in Wandsworth will be covered more fully in a separate volume of Tramway Classics. (D.Trevor Rowe)

44. Three standard gauge railway tracks were crossed on the level at the eastern end of Nine Elms Lane. Out of camera shot opposite the Southampton Arms just past the cyclist, was the original terminal building of the London and Southampton Railway. A picture appears in the Middleton Press Southern Main Lines album, *Waterloo to Woking*. (J.C.Gillham)

R I V E R
T H A M E S

Nine Elms
Pier

M u d

Railway
Wharf

14

Brunswick
(L. & S.

Wharves

Offices

L. B

P. H.

Engine
Ho.

N

P. H.

P. H.

The 1895 map at 25" to 1 mile shows the single track horse tramway. The single railway line crossing it was removed and the three-track crossing became four.

BRIDGE CARRYING
NARROW GAUGE RAILWAY
OVER ROAD

DOCK

N

SITE OF
TIDE MILL

KIRTLING STREET

PUBLIC
BATHS

CRINGLE STREET

NINE ELMS LANE

"ROYAL
RIFLEMAN"
P.H.

MILL POND
STREET BRIDGE

SITE OF
MANOR
HOUSE

CEYLON STREET

St. GEORGE'S
CHURCH

HAINES STREET

GAS WORKS

LINES BETWEEN QUEEN'S ROAD AND ALBERT EMBANKMENT RECONSTRUCTED FROM HORSE TRAMWAY AND OP

(FORMER HORSE TRAMWAY AUTHORISED BY THE "SOUTH LONDON TRAMWAYS ACT, 1879". THE LINE IN BATTERSEA PARK ROAD, FROM FAL
FIRST SECTION OF THIS COMPANY'S SYSTEM, AND WAS OPENED ON 1ST JANUARY 1881; THE CONTINUATION EASTWARD ALONG NINE EL
AUTHORISED BY THE "SOUTH LONDON TRAMWAYS ACT, 1882".)

NOTES. (PRE LONDON TRANSPORT).
ALL ELECTRIC TRAMWAYS SHOWN HEREON, L.C.C. OWNED, CONDUIT OPERATED.
OF THE FORMER HORSE TRAMWAYS, THE LONDON TRAMWAYS Cº WAS TRANSFERRED
TO THE L.C.C. ON 1ST JANUARY 1899, AND THE SOUTH LONDON TRAMWAYS Cº ON
22ND NOVEMBER 1902. AFTER TRANSFER, THE LINES WERE WORKED BY THE COUN

45. Two British Railways, Southern Region shunting tractors are propelling goods wagons across the tramtracks. The railway lines connected the North Goods Depot with Brunswick Yard and the Thames wharves. (J.H.Meredith)

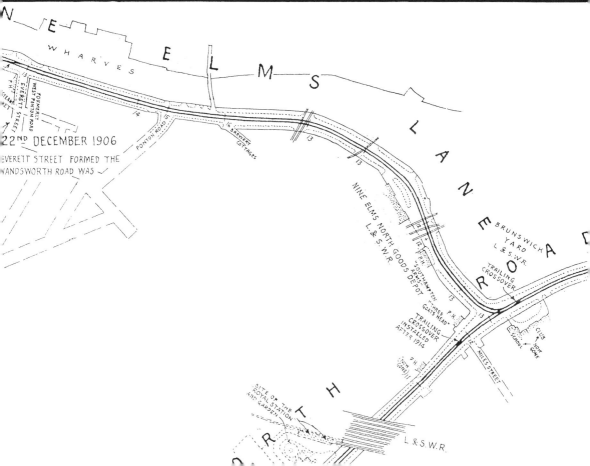

46. In the vicinity of Ponton Road and the former Nine Elms Brewery, service 12 encountered another brace of railway sidings leading away to the banks of the river. This area was subsequently totally transformed and rebuilt to accommodate commercial premises. (J.C.Gillham)

47. Car 202 takes the left hand track under the railway bridge which carried a narrow gauge line serving Nine Elms Gasworks. The tram is on the hump back Millpond Bridge. The traffic island formed a barrier to discourage motorists from overtaking tramcars. (D.A.Thompson)

5. Vauxhall to Stockwell

48. Car 2161 takes the South Lambeth Road turn away from Vauxhall. This tram formerly belonged to the London United Tramways and it once plied the trunk route from Shepherds Bush to Uxbridge. On formation of London Transport, LUT car 392 became LT car 2161. A subsequent renumbering was in store as this vehicle was later transferred to Leeds where, as car 562, it entered service in 1952, only to be withdrawn again in October 1957. The Leeds system closed in 1959 and nearly all the ex-London Feltham cars were put to the torch. (J.H.Meredith)

49. The crossover opposite Lawn Lane is beneath the tram as it releases its cargo of schoolgirls to be guided across the road by the policeman standing in the roadway in front of the railway bridge. (R.J.S.Wiseman)

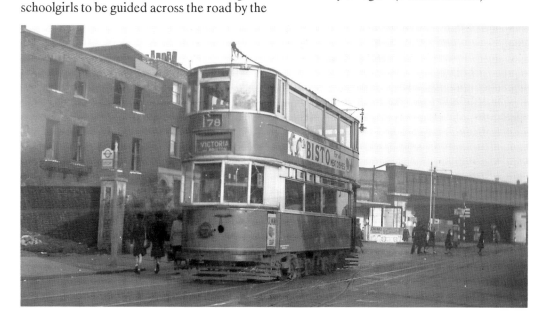

50. Some of the South London landscape could be grim. The tramcar, in splendid isolation, adds a colourful note to an otherwise uninspiring street scene. The film "Passport to Pimlico" was made in this vicinity.
(D.A.Thompson)

51. Where Lansdowne Road crosses South Lambeth Road car 1809 halts at the traffic signals. There is a faded elegance about this part of the world, and many fine buildings which have seen better days can be glimpsed behind the tram. (J.H.Meredith)

1224.—FELTHAM CARS.

The attention of all employees is called to the transfer to Streatham Depot of Feltham cars, which will operate on the undermentioned routes.

Employees must not stand between tracks on these routes whilst cars are passing.

Routes 8 and 20, Victoria to Tooting Broadway.

Via Vauxhall Cross, South Lambeth Road, Stockwell Road, Brixton Road, Streatham Hill, Mitcham Lane, Tooting Broadway, Tooting High Street, Balham High Road and Clapham Road.

Routes 16 and 18, Purley to Embankment.

Via London Road, Norbury, Streatham High Road, Brixton Road, Newington Butts, Elephant & Castle, London Road, St. George's Circus, Blackfriars Bridge, Victoria Embankment, Westminster Bridge Road and Kennington Road.

Route No. 10, City to Tooting Broadway.

Via Southwark Bridge, Marshalsea Road, Borough High Street, Newington Causeway, Kennington Park Road, Camberwell New Road, Brixton Road and Mitcham Lane.

Emergency Routes.

Waterloo Road, Borough Road, Lancaster Street, St. George's Road, Lambeth Palace Road, Albert Embankment, Harleyford Road, Oval, Harleyford Street, Lambeth Road.

52. Cars 2135 and 2128 hold centre stage as we observe service 20 on its last day of operation, 6th January 1951. Both these trams were later sold to Leeds, but car 2135 never entered revenue service in the Yorkshire town. (J.H.Meredith)

53. By Stockwell Terrace we observe a cameo of Central Road Services' operations, with car 1353 in the starring role and the STL bus playing a supporting part. (J.H.Meredith)

54. Yet another bus/tram combination a few yards on from the previous view. Note the very solid War Memorial Clock Tower raised in memory of the fallen in the First World War. In the 1920s the LCC was engaged in a battle royal with competing buses from the London General Omnibus Co.. (R.J.Harley Coll.)

55. One of the capital's most eminent transport photographers has captured the essence of tramway operation at the Swan, Stockwell. A tram waits to emerge from South Lambeth Road as a sister car sweeps down from Clapham Road. The curves in the foreground were opened in 1922 to enable service 34 to be extended. (D.A.Thompson)

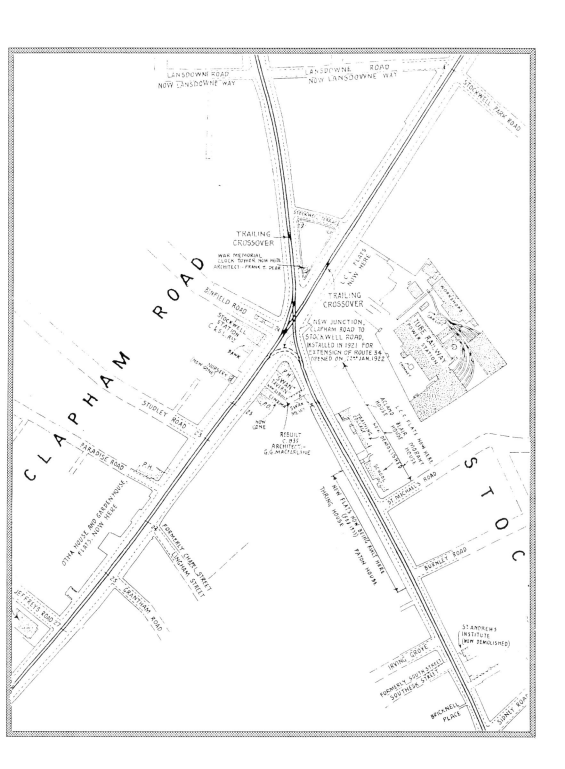

56. North of the Swan junction, car 1795 is flanked by blocks of 1930s LCC flats as it reverses on a crossover. This was a regular Saturday afternoon short working, Wimbledon to Stockwell. (J.H.Meredith)

——————▶

57. South of the junction we are treated to a kaleidoscope of period road transport. On this Saturday in October 1950 the Evening News van has just arrived with the classified football results. At the end of the season some London fans would have cause to celebrate as Spurs took the Football League championship. The only South London team in the top section, Charlton Athletic, managed a mediocre seventeenth place, but at least their fans could still travel to The Valley by tramcar. (J.H.Meredith)

——————▶

58. As motor traffic increased after the war so did the number of accidents involving trams. As illustrated here at the Swan, where car 171 makes for Stockwell Road, conflicting movements with non-railbound vehicles were not helped by the poorly placed Keep Left bollard. (C.Carter)

59. This postcard view was sent in 1904; there is a calm tranquility in turn-of-the-century Stockwell Road. The sleepy village of Stockwell came to national prominence in 1778 when lurid tales of the Stockwell "ghost" intrigued the nation. In contrast, the only spectre haunting this horse car is the new wonder of the transport world, the electric tramcar. (J.H.Price Coll.)

60. The horse cars which operated along Stockwell Road were of the "low bridge" variety similar to car 34. The London Southern Tramways Co. started to reconstruct their fleet in 1895 with the main new feature the provision of "garden" or transverse seats on the top deck. (J.H.Price Coll.)

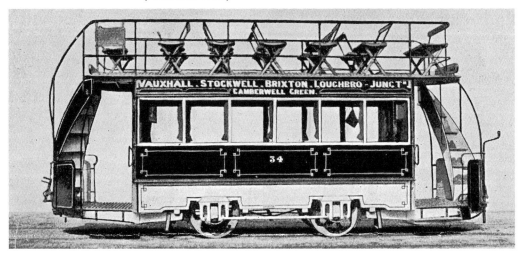

61. There was single track between Rumsey Road and Stockwell Green. Car 191 is about to squeeze past two other road users; to the right of the tram is the Old Queen's Head which was situated next door to the former horse tram depot. (Lens of Sutton)

62. The double conduit slot can clearly be seen in this picture. Car 2128 demonstrates that road space was at a premium, fortunately there are no parked cars! (J.H.Meredith)

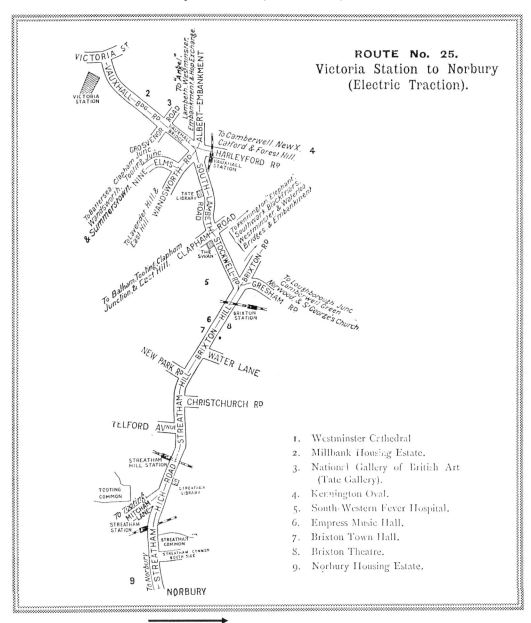

ROUTE No. 25.
Victoria Station to Norbury
(Electric Traction).

VICTORIA ST.
VAUXHALL—BOG—RD
VICTORIA STATION
2
3
To "Angel."
Lambeth, Westminster.
Embankment & Hop Exchange.
VAUXHALL BRIDGE
ALBERT—EMBANKMENT
To Camberwell. New X.
Catford & Forest Hill.
HARLEYFORD RD.
4
VAUXHALL STATION
GROSVENOR ROAD
Clapham Junc.
Tooting Junc.
ELMS—
NINE—
To Battersea,
Wandsworth,
& Summerstown.
To Lavender Hill &
East Hill.
WANDSWORTH RD
TATE LIBRARY
SOUTH—LAMBETH ROAD
CLAPHAM ROAD
STOCKWELL RD
THE SWAN
To Balham, Tooting Clapham
Junction, & East Hill.
To Kennington, Elephant,
Southwark, Blackfriars,
Westminster, & Waterloo
Bridges, & Embankment
5
BRIXTON RD.
GRESHAM RD
BRIXTON HILL
To Loughborough Junc
Camberwell Green
Norwood, & St George's Church
BRIXTON STATION
6
7
8
NEW PARK RD.
WATER LANE
BRIXTON HILL
CHRISTCHURCH RD
TELFORD AVENUE
STREATHAM HILL
STREATHAM HILL STATION
STREATHAM LIBRARY
TOOTING COMMON
To Tooting
MITCHAM LANE
STREATHAM STATION
STREATHAM HIGH ROAD
STREATHAM COMMON
STREATHAM COMMON SOUTH SIDE
To Norbury
9
NORBURY

1. Westminster Cathedral
2. Millbank Housing Estate.
3. National Gallery of British Art (Tate Gallery).
4. Kennington Oval.
5. South-Western Fever Hospital.
6. Empress Music Hall.
7. Brixton Town Hall.
8. Brixton Theatre.
9. Norbury Housing Estate.

63. A last look at Stockwell Road as car 181 prepares to enter the single track. Note the temporary tram stop by the bicycle; in a few hours this road would be served exclusively by buses. (Lens of Sutton)

6. Brixton

64. Brixton Road, Stockwell Road junction in March 1952 and the shops are beginning to fill with consumer goods. The brave new world of 1950s prosperity seemingly has no place for the tramcar and in a couple of weeks the tracks here will fall silent for ever. Following political and social trends, it is interesting to observe that a local lad, one John Major, once applied for a job on the replacing buses, he later found a more lucrative position as Prime Minister of the United Kingdom! (J.H.Meredith)

65. Brixton Road has witnessed several forms of tramway traction. First horses from 1870, then cable cars from 1892 and finally electric trams working on the conduit system from 1904. One of the original LCC four wheel cars is pictured just opposite Canterbury Road. (J.H.Price Coll.)

66. August 1907 sees the track being excavated for the new connecting lines to Stockwell Road and Gresham Road. All work of this nature was done manually by gangs of workmen, they achieved miracles with very little mechanical assistance. In the centre of the photo rails have been left as an access track for horse cars. (LCC official photo)

67. From the standpoint of Brixton Station railway bridge we look north past the well known local store, Quin & Axtens. (J.H.Price Coll.)

68. Further along Brixton Road by the main shopping centre, a rebuilt C class tramcar slides past a chap with a sandwich board. The nearest bridge carries the newly electrified South London Line. The Middleton Press album of that name reveals the dramatic competition between the two forms of electric transport. (R.J.Harley Coll.)

69. Acre Lane, Brixton meets the main road and joins Effra Road at the junction outside Lambeth Town Hall. Car 381, formerly owned by Croydon Corporation, sets course for home territory. (C.Carter)

70. "They shall not pass"...On 30th September 1950 a lorry straddles the road blocking both tram tracks. Smashed carboys on the highway suggest a caustic spillage. There was no alternative but to wait for the fire brigade to remove the obstacle and hose the whole lot down. (R.J.S.Wiseman)

71. Brixton Road by Angell Road crossover and car 2155 is on the long haul from the Embankment to Purley. Again it is difficult, in the light of contemporary congestion problems, to imagine a time when Brixton Road wasn't filled with lines of traffic. (J.H.Meredith)

72. Car 1441 was completely rebuilt in February 1933, after which it was allocated to Streatham Depot. Here it is caught on camera in Brixton Road around 1937. (G.N.Southerden)

7. Vauxhall to Kennington

73. Outbound to Forest Hill, car 1537 leaves Vauxhall to journey along Harleyford Road towards Kennington Oval. (J.H.Meredith)

74. The Oval, home of Surrey County Cricket Club, was opened in April 1846. Trams passed the southern boundary walls and top deck passengers could often share for a few fleeting minutes a grandstand view of the events taking place on the pitch. The legendary batsman, Jack Hobbs, was a frequent passenger on the LCC trams in between scoring numerous centuries. (J.H.Meredith)

75. A line of vehicles waits for the lights in Harleyford Street by Kennington Oval tube station. (R.J.S.Wiseman)

76. On 3rd June 1933 car 1370 overturned at Kennington, the tram was badly damaged and the insurance money was used to rebuild car 1446, which was then renumbered 1370. However, that was not the end of the story, as parts salvaged from the supposed "write off" were employed in the construction of a new tram, car 2. (R.J.Harley Coll.)

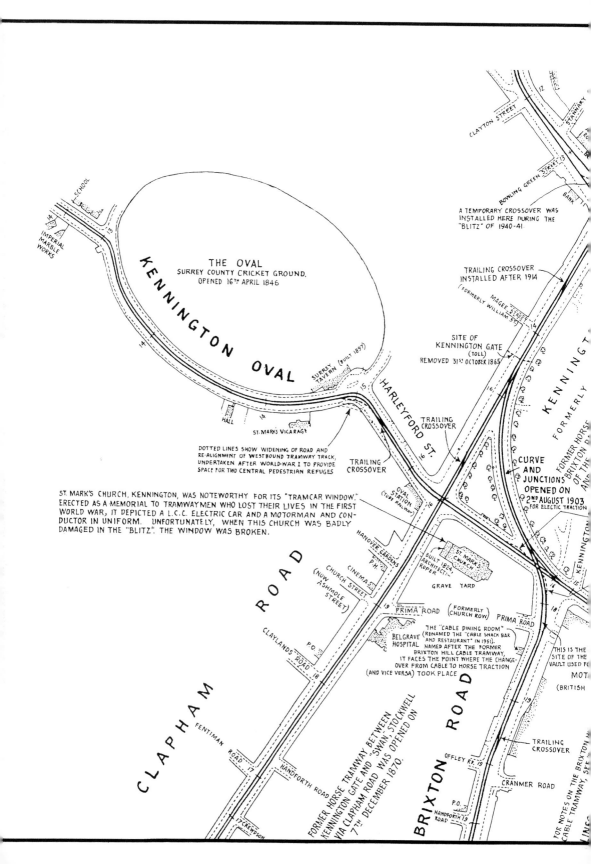

THE OVAL
SURREY COUNTY CRICKET GROUND.
OPENED 16TH APRIL 1846

KENNINGTON OVAL

IMPERIAL MARBLE WORKS

SCHOOL

SURREY TAVERN (BUILT 1897)

HALL

ST. MARK'S VICARAGE

HARLEYFORD ST.

A TEMPORARY CROSSOVER WAS INSTALLED HERE DURING THE "BLITZ" OF 1940-41

TRAILING CROSSOVER INSTALLED AFTER 1914
(FORMERLY WILLIAM ST.)

MAGEE STREET
(FORMERLY WILLIAM ST.)

SITE OF KENNINGTON GATE (TOLL)
REMOVED 31ST OCTOBER 1865

CLAYTON STREET

BOWLING GREEN STREET

STANNARY

BANK

KENNINGT

FORMERLY

FORMER HORSE
BRIXTON
OF THE

TRAILING CROSSOVER

TRAILING CROSSOVER

DOTTED LINES SHOW WIDENING OF ROAD AND RE-ALIGNMENT OF WESTBOUND TRAMWAY TRACK, UNDERTAKEN AFTER WORLD-WAR I TO PROVIDE SPACE FOR TWO CENTRAL PEDESTRIAN REFUGES

CURVE AND JUNCTIONS OPENED ON 2ND AUGUST 1903 FOR ELECTRIC TRACTION

ST. MARK'S CHURCH, KENNINGTON, WAS NOTEWORTHY FOR ITS "TRAMCAR WINDOW." ERECTED AS A MEMORIAL TO TRAMWAYMEN WHO LOST THEIR LIVES IN THE FIRST WORLD WAR, IT DEPICTED A L.C.C. ELECTRIC CAR AND A MOTORMAN AND CONDUCTOR IN UNIFORM. UNFORTUNATELY, WHEN THIS CHURCH WAS BADLY DAMAGED IN THE "BLITZ", THE WINDOW WAS BROKEN.

OVAL STATION (TUBE RAILWAY)

HANOVER GARDENS P.H.

ST. MARK'S CHURCH
BUILT 1824. ARCHITECT: ROPER

GRAVE YARD

KENNINGTON

CLAPHAM ROAD

CHURCH STREET (NOW ASHMOLE STREET)

CINEMA ST.

CLAYLANDS ROAD

P.O.

PRIMA ROAD (FORMERLY CHURCH ROW) PRIMA ROAD

BELGRAVE HOSPITAL

THE "CABLE DINING ROOM" (RENAMED THE "CABLE SNACK BAR AND RESTAURANT" IN 1951). NAMED AFTER THE FORMER BRIXTON HILL CABLE TRAMWAY, IT FACES THE POINT WHERE THE CHANGE-OVER FROM CABLE TO HORSE TRACTION (AND VICE VERSA) TOOK PLACE

THIS IS THE SITE OF THE VAULT USED FO

MOT

(BRITISH

FENTIMAN ROAD

HANDFORTH ROAD

FORMER HORSE TRAMWAY BETWEEN KENNINGTON GATE AND "SWAN." STOCKWELL VIA CLAPHAM ROAD WAS OPENED ON 7TH DECEMBER 1870.

BRIXTON ROAD

OFFLEY RD.

CRANMER ROAD

P.O.

HANDFORTH ROAD

CREWDSON

TRAILING CROSSOVER

FOR NOTES ON THE BRIXTON SEE

CABLE TRAMWAY,

K

MMON

HORNS" AND
THE FIRST SECTION
AMWAYS CO'S LINES
1870.

NES SHOW LATER TRACK DIVERSIONS
T THE ERECTION OF CENTRAL
AN REFUGES.

M B E R W E L L

TRAILING
CROSSOVER

ST. MARK'S ROAD
(NOW
HILLINGDON
STREET)

N E W   R O A D

FOXLEY
ROAD

PH

"SKINNERS ARMS"

13

14

DUGDALE ST.

77. At the end of Harleyford Street car 1628 is
about to cross over the lines going south into
Clapham Road and north into Kennington
Park Road. (D.A.Thompson)

78. We shift our vantage point a few yards from
the previous view to catch sight of car 1828
waiting at the lights in Clapham Road.
(R.J.S.Wiseman)

79. St.Mark's Church, Kennington dates from the 1820s and it is one of the places of worship constructed as a thanksgiving for the victory at Waterloo in 1815. One famous son of Kennington was Viscount Montgomery of Alamein, whose father was once vicar of St.Mark's. (J.B.Gent Coll.)

80. An early print of a horse car passing St.Mark's Church shows that the top deck was a male preserve and, according to the conventions of the time, ladies would never be expected to ascend the metal staircase. (R.J.Harley Coll.)

81. The lower saloon of the 1870 horse cars is depicted here in this contemporary etching. The well dressed Victorian travellers sitting facing one another rather imply that the "working class was evicted to sit outside to endure the elements. (C.Durand. Illustrated London News)

82. Above ground electric traction manifests itself in the form of the tramcar, seen here by the Oval Station. Below ground the City and South London Railway, opened in 1890, pioneered this form of city transport which has performed such sterling service for Londoners. This tube railway was later incorporated into the Northern Line. (R.J.S.Wiseman)

83. At Kennington Park Road, Camberwell New Road crossing, car 1845 coasts over the junction. (J.H.Meredith)

84. Car 1810 has just reached the crossover north of the Oval Station. This layout was useful in emergencies for short working trams. (J.H.Meredith)

85. Before wartime destruction and the blocks of flats built by the LCC in the 1930s, this picture shows trailer car T26 on the Merton to Embankment service and the date is around 1921. (J.H.Price Coll.)

86. Car 2095 has been diverted to Kennington because of an obstruction along its normal route, South Lambeth Road. The RT bus on the right is emerging from the northern end of Brixton Road. (J.H.Meredith)

87. Over forty years earlier than the previous photo, but taken at the same location, we witness car 96 en route to Tooting. (J.H.Price Coll.)

88. This postcard was sent in March 1907 at a period when top covers were being fitted to the LCC fleet. The rationale behind this was to maximise earnings and increase passenger comfort during bad weather when, not unnaturally, only a few hardy souls would venture on to the top deck. It is ironic that at the end of the twentieth century the average speed of London's traffic matches that achieved by the horse buses depicted here. The trams, of course, could easily outpace their horse bus rivals! (J.H.Price Coll.)

89. The waiting shelter is conveniently situated at the tramway junction in this scene from Edwardian days. This stretch of road was once called Kennington Gate after the toll gate which was removed in 1865. (J.B.Gent Coll.)

90. The pointsman's hand is just visible behind the traffic light, as he switches car 1928, on service 72 to Woolwich, into Brixton Road in 1950. (J.H.Meredith)

← 91. Car 961, with body bracing on the lower deck to prolong its working life, rumbles over the Brixton Road, Camberwell New Road spur on 12th December 1950. (J.H.Meredith)

← 92. As the bus conversion programme proceeded, so scenes like this became more common on once tram dominated roads. Car 1387 is easily outnumbered as it makes the turn into Camberwell New Road. (D.A.Thompson)

93. The tram on service 33 is about to come straight towards the photographer who is standing on a pedestrian island, situated between the tram tracks, in Brixton Road in 1952. (J.C.Gillham)

94. We look now in a southeasterly direction as car 838 halts outside the imposing building of the General Motor Cab Company. Near this spot was the original changeover from horse to cable traction for the line along Brixton Road to Streatham. (R.J.Harley Coll.)

95. Camberwell New Road connects Kennington with Camberwell and the view here is taken from the corner of Vassall Road with the Union Tavern on the right. (A.J.Watkins Coll.)

96. North of the old Kennington Gate and just before the Horns Tavern, car 1802 reverses; again this is on a diversion due to trouble in South Lambeth Road. (J.H.Meredith)

97. A flag flutters over the Horns Tavern in tribute to a bygone Kennington evoked by this splendid street scene. In those days it was still possible to enjoy a leisurely stroll across the road without being knocked down by stray motor cars or asphyxiated by petrol fumes. (J.B.Gent Coll.)

98. The Horns Tavern again provides the backdrop for this 1950 scene. Car 1908 takes the straight route up Kennington Park Road to the Elephant, whilst a sister car waits to emerge from Kennington Road. (J.H.Meredith)

99. In the last week of London's trams, car 1911 slows outside the one time Assembly Rooms which were "blitzed" in the Second World War. (R.J.S.Wiseman)

100. By the Horns Tavern in Kennington Road a temporary crossover was inserted around 1940-41 to act as an emergency reversal point in the event of streets being blocked by bomb damage. In this June 1952 view the course of this trackwork is clearly visible. (J.C.Gillham)

101. We catch a final look at Kennington Road with a tram passing a compulsory LT stop sign fixed to a concrete post. This was the second style of stop sign introduced by London Transport. (J.C.Gillham)

102. The final leg of our journey takes us along Kennington Park Road in the direction of the Elephant and Castle. The LCC pointsman, on the left of the picture, looks towards the camera, as trailer car T64 heads north. Trailers were used on some services from 1913-1923. (J.B.Gent Coll.)

103. The area around Kennington was once associated with the youthful Charlie Chaplin, the great silent film comedian. Kennington Theatre to the right of the tram formerly catered for a range of tastes ranging from popular music hall variety to the classics. (J.H.Price Coll.)

104. Car 825 is in Kennington Park Road in the vicinity of Cottington Road. Pre-bottled milk transport is on the right. (J.B.Gent Coll.)

105. The end of our tram ride takes place in Newington Butts, with the Elephant and Castle junction in view. This area is fully described in companion volume, *Southwark and Deptford Tramways*. (J.H.Meredith)

8. Rolling Stock

The C class, numbered 202-301, was built by Brush in 1903. These four wheel cars on Brill 21E trucks proved more solidly constructed than the similar B class cars. They were originally delivered in open top condition with reversed stairs. Passengers in the lower saloon sat on long benches facing one another; on the top deck transverse seats were arranged in two rows of double seats with no provision for a trolley standard as all C class vehicles worked exclusively on conduit equipped lines. From around 1905 roof covers began to be fitted to these trams with the reversed stairs retained. At first the open balconies were kept and the vehicles thus converted were allocated to class C/1. All enclosed top covers then made their appearance and picture 68 illustrates a car in this condition, it was classified C/2. Direct stairs were fitted to all cars in classes A-D in a programme lasting 1906-1911.

Powerful magnetic brakes were subsequently fitted to C class cars and many of this type worked the steep Dog Kennel Hill. They gave fine service for many years until by 1930 all had been replaced by new eight wheel trams of classes HR/2 and E/3.

106. The class as built, showing the reversed stairs and open top deck; the car is painted in the standard LCC purple lake and primrose with the fleet numbers and LCC lettering in gold. (LCC official photo)

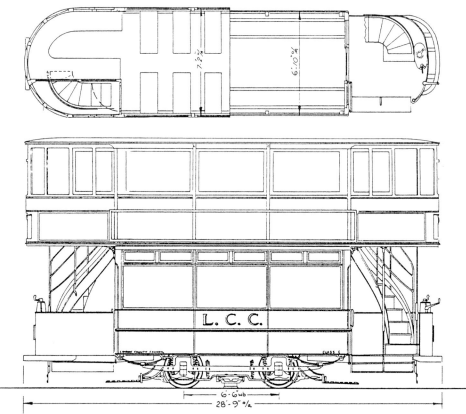

107. Seen in the 1920s at Greenwich, this C class car is working service 68 to Waterloo. It is shown in final condition. (D.A.Thompson Coll.)

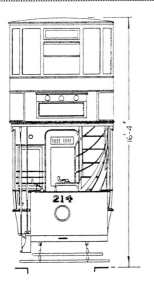

108. Services over Dog Kennel Hill were operated by this class with help from LCC M class cars until the arrival of the new HR/2 type trams. Here car 240 takes a rest from its duties at Blackwall Tunnel, South Side terminus. (G.N.Southerden)

SCALE
FEET 0   3   6   9   12

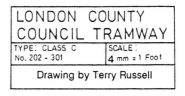

LONDON COUNTY
COUNCIL TRAMWAY

TYPE: CLASS C	SCALE:
No. 202 - 301	4 mm = 1 Foot
Drawing by Terry Russell	

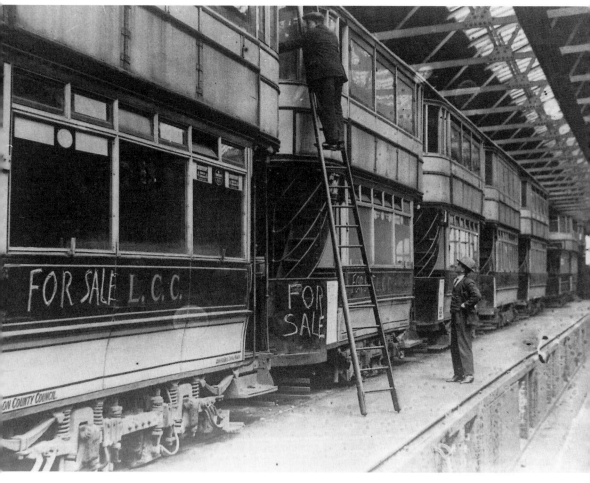

109. The chalked inscriptions tell the story. Each of these vehicles, here pictured in Chiswick Depot around 1930, could be acquired for the princely sum of just £5. (LCC official photo)

9. Request Stops

Before the age of mechanised public transport, horse buses and trams stopped virtually anywhere to pick up or set down passengers. The faster electric trams required fixed stopping places and these were generally indicated by metal signs. At certain locations where more customers could be expected, compulsory stops were instituted, normally with the message ALL CARS STOP HERE. Also at steep gradients and sharp bends, trams were sometimes required by law to halt before proceeding, these Board of Trade stops, as they were known, were common on British tramways. Request stops, which are the subject of this study, were provided for the convenience of passengers and the LCC applied for Parliamentary powers to use them in 1908. A signal had to given to the conductor and driver, normally by pressing a bell, that a passenger wished to alight at the next request stop. At the roadside an outstretched arm or a waved umbrella or newspaper were usually sufficient to attract the attention of the oncoming motorman.

The author would like to thank John Gillham who had the forethought to record these items of "street furniture" before they disappeared from the London scene.

111. This is an example of the LCC vertical type sign, it is attached to an iron post situated outside Lambeth North Station in Kennington Road. (J.C.Gillham)

110. Although London Transport had been in business since 1933, certain request stops from the LCC era escaped their clutches and managed to survive almost to the last day of tramway operation. Here at the top of Academy Road, Woolwich an LCC clover leaf sign is pictured in June 1952. The white lettering is on a red background with a blue painted STOP on a white field. Note the seat thoughfully provided by Woolwich Borough Council, it was painted medium green with W.B.C picked out in gold letters. (J.C.Gillham)

112. The LCC horizontal type is featured here at Peckham High Road by Sumner Avenue. (J.C.Gillham)

113. This stop in Lee High Road is fixed to a rather ornate gas lamp bracket. This location appears again in *Lewisham and Catford Tramways*, picture 48. The request stop is in the style of the LUT, MET company signs; the bar containing the word TRAMWAYS was blue on a red circle. TRAMS STOP BY REQUEST was in black on a cream background. (J.C.Gillham)

114. At Eltham Road by Sutcliffe Park, the request stop has been fixed to a traction standard. Obviously this was the preferred method where overhead wires were employed, otherwise the LCC and later LT had powers to attach signs to other items of street furniture such as lamp standards. (J.C.Gillham)

115. At the corner of Kidbrooke Park Road and Eltham Road, the first style of LT request stop is seen attached to a concrete post. (J.C.Gillham)

116. On the second LT style the word TRAMWAYS has been slimmed down to TRAM. This stop is near the Bricklayers Arms in the Old Kent Road. (J.C.Gillham)

117. For most people this style needs no introduction and the shape must be known the world over. However, unlike the present day bus stop with its red background, the white bull's eye is on a blue background in this final tram version of the LT request stop. (J.C.Gillham)

ALTERATIONS TO STOPS.

2012.—VAUXHALL CROSS.

IN NEW ROAD.

Westbound.
 Trams to stop at Lamp Standard No. H.897, as at present.

IN HARLEYFORD ROAD.

South-east bound.
 Trams to stop by request at Lamp Standard No. 170.
 Buses to stop opposite No. 18, as at present.·
The North-west bound tram and bus stops are abolished.

IN SOUTH LAMBETH ROAD.

Northbound.
 Trams to stop at the Southern pillar of the Northern entrance to No. 38 (The Vulite Co., Ltd.).
 Buses to stop at the Lamp Standard outside No. 46.

Southbound.
 Trams to stop opposite No. 46, as at present.
 Buses to stop opposite the garage (No. 42). as at present.

IN PARRY STREET.

Westbound.
 Trams to stop by request at Lamp Standard No. H.908.
 Buses to stop at Lamp Standard No. H.906.

IN WANDSWORTH ROAD.

Northbound.
 Trams to stop at the Central Island, as at present.

Northbound Buses.
  (1) Ten yards south of Lamp Standard No. 437 (Routes 136-236).
  (2) At Lamp Standard No. 438 (Routes 32-88).
  (3) Opposite the party-wall of Nos. 37/39 (Routes 77-77a).

118. Have stop will travel! Temporary "dolly"
stops fixed to round concrete bases were used
by London Transport in the transition period
before the gleaming new bus stops could be
unveiled. Here the gentleman enthusiast is
making his own political point at the top of Dog
Kennel Hill. (J.H.Price)

10. Finale

119. We are told that all good things must come to an end, but the London tramway system deserved better than the fate of car 1990 on its last run from Victoria. (A.J.Watkins Coll.)

120. Hail the conquering bus! RTL 1260 on a tramway replacement edges past the tracks being torn up in Stockwell Road. Will we ever see a modern tramway system to cater for South London's needs? (D.Trevor Rowe)

96